THE HEINZ BOOK OF BAKED BEAN RECIPES

Colour Library Books

HEINZ BEANS: INTRODUCTION

We all know that Heinz baked beans taste great, but did you know just how good they are for you?

The beans we know have an ancient and varied history. First eaten nearly 9,000 years ago, they have been put to many uses since. In the Middle Ages, for example, crushed beans and garlic were believed to cure colds and coughs.

Today we eat baked beans for more simple reasons. They taste delicious, are extremely nutritious and offer great value for money. Maybe that is why over 400 million cans are eaten every year by the British alone! Beans are packed full with protein and fibre but are still surprisingly low in calories and they help to make a great meal whether you just want a snack, such as beans on toast, or something more filling.

Heinz, makers of Britain's most famous baked beans, have compiled this mouthwatering selection of recipes which offer you 30 menu suggestions including quick snacks, meals for kids, salads and casseroles.

The Heinz range of beans includes Beans with Sausages, Curried Beans with Sultanas, Barbeque Beans, Bean St Kids and, of course, Britain's favourite, Heinz Baked Beans. The recipes in this book have been put together using just some of these varieties to show you how very versatile beans can be. We hope that you will enjoy such tasty dishes as Chilled Tomato and Bean Soup, Spicy Pasta and Prawns and even Bean Cheesecake. Once you have tried all these recipes, why not try creating some of your own? All it takes is imagination and a tin of your favourite beans!

Photography by Peter Barry
Recipes Prepared and Styled by Bridgeen Deery and Wendy Devenish
Designed by Dick Richardson

CLB 2024
© 1989 Colour Library Books Ltd., Godalming, Surrey.
Printed in Belgium by Casterman.
All rights reserved.
ISBN 0 86283 761 8

CHILLED TOMATO AND BEAN SOUP

SERVES 4

Chilled soups are really delicious in summer and they are amongst the simplest of starters to make. Try this variation on the traditional Spanish soup, Gazpacho.

1 x 397g/14oz can tomatoes in natural juice
1 clove garlic, crushed
1 x 450g/15.9oz can Heinz Baked Beans
½ a cucumber, seeded and chopped
1 red pepper, seeded and chopped
275ml/½ pint chicken stock
4 tbsps olive oil
Salt and freshly ground black pepper

To Serve
Thin slices of red or green pepper
Thinly sliced onion rings
Chopped cucumber
Fried bread croutons
Parsley, or spring onions, chopped

1. Put the canned tomatoes, garlic, baked beans, chopped cucumber, red pepper and chicken stock into a liquidiser and blend until smooth.

STEP 1

2. Add the olive oil and salt and pepper to taste. If the soup is too thick for your liking, add a little extra chicken stock.

STEP 2

3. Chill the soup very thoroughly for 3-4 hours before serving.

4. Serve in small bowls, with an ice cube floated in each one, and accompanied by slices of pepper, onion rings, chopped cucumber and croutons. Sprinkle the soup with the parsley, or spring onions.

Cook's Notes

TIME: Preparation takes 20 minutes, plus a minimum of 4 hours chilling time.

VARIATION: The amount of garlic may be varied or omitted altogether, to suit your taste.

COOK'S TIP: The oil must be added in a thin, steady stream. If added too quickly, the soup will curdle.

CURRIED BEAN AND APPLE SOUP

SERVES 4-6

A delicious and refreshing soup recipe from Heinz Beans, this Curried Bean and Apple Soup can be served hot or chilled. Served chilled, it makes an ideal starter for a light summer lunch.

25g/1oz butter, or margarine
1 medium onion, chopped
450g/1lb cooking apples, peeled, cored and
    chopped
2 x 225g/7.94oz cans Heinz Curried Beans with
    Sultanas
575ml/1 pint water
1 chicken stock cube
Salt and pepper

---

1. Melt the butter and fry the onion, until transparent.

STEP 1

2. Add the apples, the contents of 1½ cans beans, the water and stock cube. Bring to the boil, reduce the heat, cover and simmer for 20 minutes.

STEP 2

3. Allow to cool slightly, then purée in a liquidiser until smooth.

STEP 3

4. Return the soup to the pan, add the reserved beans and heat through, if serving hot. Add salt and pepper to taste. If serving cold, allow soup to cool and then chill, preferably overnight, in the refrigerator.

5. If wished, garnish with croutons or thinly sliced pieces of apple before serving.

Cook's Notes

⤶ TIME: Preparation takes about 15 minutes and cooking takes about 25-30 minutes.

🍞 COOK'S TIP: If you don't have a liquidiser, push the mixture through a wire sieve, using a wooden spoon.

❗ WATCHPOINT: Remove the croutons from the hot fat when barely brown, as they continue to cook slightly, whilst draining. Serve them at the last moment, otherwise they will go soggy.

EGG DIPPED FRIED BREAD

SERVES 4

Take fried bread one step further. This recipe uses cream and mushrooms and makes a delicious light lunch or tea.

---

2 eggs
3 tbsps single cream
Salt and freshly ground black pepper
8 small slices bread
12 small, flat mushrooms
Oil, or butter
2 x 450g/15.9oz cans Heinz Baked Beans
75g/3oz cheese, grated
Sprigs of parsley or watercress, to garnish

---

1. Beat the eggs with the cream and salt and pepper to taste.

2. Trim the mushroom stalks. Brush caps with oil and grill for 3-4 minutes, until just tender.

3. Heat the baked beans through gently, in a saucepan.

4. Trim the crusts from the bread. Dip each slice into the beaten egg mixture, allowing any excess to drip off.

5. Heat oil, or butter, in a pan. Lower each slice carefully into the pan and shallow-fry, turning once, until lightly golden on both sides.

6. Place the slices of egg-fried bread onto the rack of a grill pan. Top firstly with the baked beans and then with the mushrooms. Sprinkle with the grated cheese.

7. Pop under a hot grill for 1-2 minutes. Garnish with parsley, or watercress.

Cook's Notes

TIME: Preparation takes about 10 minutes and cooking takes about 15 minutes.

VARIATION: Dried mushrooms may be used instead of flat or button mushrooms. Soak the dried mushrooms in boiling water for 5 minutes and then slice them thinly.

CURRIED BEAN AND EGG MAYONNAISE

SERVES 6

Add a taste of the Orient to your table with this delicious cold dish which is full of flavour and easy to prepare.

200ml/7 fl oz mayonnaise
2 x 225g/7.94oz cans Heinz Curried Beans with
    Sultanas
Juice and grated rind ½ lemon
175g/6oz cooked chicken, cut into thin strips
    (smoked chicken could also be used)
Salt and freshly ground pepper
Finely shredded lettuce
6 hard-boiled eggs, shelled
Paprika, or curry powder
Watercress, parsley or chives, to garnish

1. Mix the mayonnaise with the curried beans and lemon juice and rind.

STEP 1

2. Stir in the chicken and add salt and pepper to taste.

STEP 2

3. Arrange a bed of shredded lettuce on a serving dish. Arrange the eggs on top.

STEP 3

4. Spoon the mayonnaise and bean mixture over and around the eggs. Sprinkle with paprika, or curry powder.

5. Garnish with watercress, parsley or chives, as preferred.

Cook's Notes

TIME: Preparation takes about 20 minutes. It takes 9–10 minutes to hard-boil the eggs and the dish takes about 10 minutes to assemble.

SERVING IDEAS: To make this dish into a filling main course, serve it with rolls or brown bread.

VARIATION: Substitute duck for the chicken to make it into a special occasion dish.

COOK'S TIP: If you keep the hard-boiled eggs in water, until needed, it will prevent a grey ring forming around the yolk.

BEAN AND KIDNEY SAUTÉ

SERVES 1

Shopping for, and planning, meals for one can be a problem, but the 225g/7.94oz cans of baked and curried beans are the perfect size for a single serving. So, next time you're on your own, spoil yourself with this special meal for one!

1 small onion, finely chopped
25g/1oz butter, or margarine
1 clove garlic, crushed
3 lambs' kidneys, skinned, halved and cored
Seasoned flour
150ml/¼ pint chicken stock
2 tbsps medium dry sherry
Chopped fresh rosemary, to taste
1 x 225g/7.94oz can Heinz Baked Beans

1. Fry the onion gently in the butter for 4 minutes.

2. Add the garlic and the kidneys, dusted in seasoned flour, and fry gently, until the kidneys are sealed on all sides.

STEP 2

3. Add the stock, sherry and rosemary gradually and simmer gently for 8 minutes

STEP 3

4. Stir in the baked beans carefully and heat through.

STEP 4

5. Serve with hot crusty bread, or a baked jacket potato, and a mixed salad.

Cook's Notes

⤴ TIME: Preparation takes about 20 minutes and cooking takes about 25-30 minutes.

◆ PREPARATION: After skinning, halving and coring the kidneys, soak them in water and vinegar for an hour, to soften them and to lessen their strong flavour.

❗ WATCHPOINT: Do not allow the onions to brown too much, as this will make them taste bitter.

BEAN BITES

SERVES 4

These fun, bite-sized snacks are quick and easy to make and the kids will enjoy them too!

4 large slices of bread
Oil, for frying
2 x 225g/7.94oz cans Heinz Beans with Pork
    Sausages
4 tbsps grated Cheddar cheese
Small chunks cucumber
Pitted black or green olives
Cocktail sticks

1. Cut two shapes, hearts, triangles, etc., from each slice of bread, with pastry cutters.

2. Fry in hot oil, until crisp and golden. Drain thoroughly on absorbent paper.

3. Sprinkle the grated cheese onto the fried bread croutes and pop them under a moderately hot grill. At the same time, heat the beans and pork sausages through and drain off any excess juice.

4. Put the beans and sausages onto the cheesy croutes and garnish with the cucumber and olives, spiked onto cocktail sticks. Serve immediately.

Cook's Notes

🕒 TIME: Preparation takes about 8 minutes and cooking takes about 10 minutes.

❓ VARIATION: An alternative garnish for the dish would be fried button mushrooms with cubes of sweet red pepper.

BEAN BURGERS

SERVES 4

When the children are on school holidays, just how do you cope with all those hungry mouths and extra meals? Kids always love burgers, so try making this quick and filling meal.

450g/1lb minced beef, or lamb
Salt and freshly ground black pepper
1 clove garlic, crushed (optional)
2 tbsps chopped parsley
1 tsp French mustard
1 x 450g/15.9oz can Heinz Baked Beans
Oil, or melted butter
4 baps, halved and lightly toasted, or poppy
    seed rolls, split
Lettuce
Sliced tomatoes
Relish or ketchup

1. Mix the minced beef with salt and pepper to taste, the garlic, if using, parsley and mustard. Mix together thoroughly.

STEP 1

2. Beat the baked beans and their sauce to a 'mush'. Mix into the minced meat mixture.

STEP 2

3. Shape into 4 thick burgers. Chill for 1 hour.

STEP 3

4. Brush the burgers with oil, or melted butter, and grill for about 5 minutes on each side.

STEP 4

5. Serve the cooked burgers in split baps or rolls, with a spoonful of relish or ketchup and garnished with lettuce and tomato.

Cook's Notes

TIME: Preparation takes about 10 minutes and cooking takes about 40 minutes.

VARIATION: Other seasonings, such as herbs, spices or breadcrumbs bound with egg, may be used to enhance the flavour of the burgers.

COOK'S TIP: Check that the burgers are cooked through, by piercing the side of the burger with a sharp knife, and increase the cooking time, if necessary.

FREEZING: Cool burgers and then stack them individually between waxed paper. Label them and then freeze for up to 3 months. Allow to defrost in the refrigerator, before cooking.

BEAN AND CHEESE LOAF

SERVES 6

Vegetarians everywhere appreciate the value of beans as an important source of protein and fibre. This tasty and nutritious dish should not only please them, but also appeal to non-vegetarians. The loaf can either be served cold, with salad, or hot, with a tomato sauce and baked jacket potatoes.

1 x 227g/8oz packet sage and onion stuffing mix
225ml/8 fl oz boiling water
1 x 450g/15.9oz can Heinz Baked Beans
Salt and freshly ground black pepper
1 egg, beaten
2 tbsps cream
75g/3oz chopped nuts

Topping
Sliced tomato and grated cheese

1. Grease and line the base of a medium-sized loaf tin.

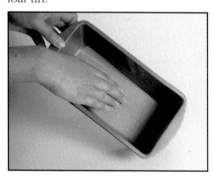

STEP 1

2. Combine the stuffing mix with the boiling water. Add this to the baked beans, salt and pepper to taste, beaten egg, cream and chopped nuts.

3. Put the mixture into the prepared loaf tin, smoothing the top level.

STEP 3

4. Cover with a piece of greased foil. Bake at 190°C/375°F/Gas Mark 5 for 45 minutes.

STEP 4

5. Turn the loaf out carefully. Top it with a layer of sliced tomato and grated cheese and return it to the oven for about 8-10 minutes.

Cook's Notes

⌕ TIME: Preparation takes about 15 minutes and cooking takes about 55 minutes.

✱ FREEZING: Cool and freeze the loaf in the dish. Pack it securely, label and freeze for up to 3 months. Allow the loaf to defrost in the refrigerator.

BEAN AND COTTAGE CHEESE PANCAKES

SERVES 4-6

Pancakes are usually associated with Shrove Tuesday, but these bean and cottage cheese pancakes taste great all the year round.

100g/4oz plain flour
Salt
1 egg
150ml/¼ pint water
150ml/¼ pint milk
1 tsp dried dill
Oil

Filling

225g/8oz cottage cheese
Salt and freshly ground black pepper
2 x 225g/7.94oz cans Heinz Curried Beans with
   Sultanas

Topping

150ml/¼ pint soured cream
Dill, dried or fresh

1. To make the batter, sieve the flour and salt into a bowl. Make a well in the centre. Add the egg and half the water and beat to a smooth paste. Whisk in the remaining water and the milk gradually. Add the dill and salt and pepper to taste. Cover the batter and leave to stand for 30 minutes.

STEP 1

2. Lightly oil a small pancake pan, about 15cm/6 inches in diameter, or even slightly smaller. Add a spoonful of batter, sufficient to give a thin, even coating, to the pan and cook, until lightly golden on the underside.

STEP 2

3. Flip the pancake over and cook on the other side. Repeat with the remaining batter, until you have about 16 small pancakes.

4. Season the cottage cheese with salt and pepper to taste and mix with the curried beans. Divide the bean and cheese mixture amongst the pancakes and roll them up.

5. Arrange on a greased, ovenproof serving dish and cover with foil. Pop into a moderately hot oven, 180°C/350°F/Gas Mark 4, for about 8 minutes.

6. Meanwhile, heat the soured cream through over a gentle heat. Spoon the soured cream down the centre of the pancakes and sprinkle with the dried, or fresh, dill.

7. Alternatively, the pancakes can be served cold. Roll the cool pancakes around the filling, arrange on a serving dish, top with a thick ribbon of cold, soured cream and sprinkle with dill.

Cook's Notes

TIME: Preparation takes about 30 minutes and cooking also takes about 30 minutes.

WATCHPOINT: Do not allow the sour cream to boil, or it will curdle.

FREEZING: Allow the pancakes to cool completely, before stacking them individually between waxed paper. Place the stacked pancakes in freezer bags, label them and freeze for up to 3 months. Defrost the pancakes completely, before separating them and reheating, as required.

BEAN AND VEGETABLE FLAN

SERVES 4-6

It is always useful to have new recipe ideas for picnics and other outdoor meals. This delicious flan recipe from Heinz is packed with nutritious vegetables and beans and is ideal for picnics.

100g/4oz plain flour
Pinch salt
25g/1oz each lard and margarine
Water
25g/1oz margarine
100g/4oz carrots, diced
100g/4oz onion, chopped
2 eggs
1 x 450g/15.9oz can Heinz Baked Beans
1/2 tsp dried thyme
Salt and pepper

1. Sift the flour and salt together and rub in the fats, until the mixture resembles fine breadcrumbs. Add sufficient water to mix to a manageable dough. Roll out on a lightly floured surface and use to line a 20cm/8 inch flan or sandwich tin.

2. Melt the margarine and fry the carrots and onions, until the onions are soft, then leave on one side to cool.

3. Beat the eggs, stir in the baked beans and thyme and season generously. Stir in the cooled vegetables and pour the mixture into the pastry case.

4. Bake in the oven at 190°C/375°F/Gas Mark 5 for about 45 minutes, until firm to the touch. Serve warm or cold, with salad or green vegetables.

Cook's Notes

TIME: Preparation takes about 40 minutes and cooking takes about 45 minutes.

VARIATION: Use different vegetables, according to the season.

SERVING IDEAS: Serve this dish, cut into thin wedges, as a starter. Alternatively, serve the flan hot or cold with a salad or green vegetables as a light meal.

FREEZING: The pastry may be made in advance, wrapped well, labelled and frozen for up to 3 months. Before using, defrost at room temperature.

NOODLES WITH BEAN SAUCE

SERVES 4

Pasta and Heinz Beans may seem an unusual combination, but, in fact, they go very well together. Beans form a ready-made sauce for pasta and a variety of other ingredients can be added for extra flavour and colour.

350g/12oz green noodles
Salt and freshly ground black pepper
4 tbsps olive oil
4 spring onions, chopped
4 rashers lean bacon, cut into strips
1 clove garlic, crushed (optional)
1 x 450g/15.9oz can Heinz Baked Beans
Grated Parmesan cheese

---

1. Cook the noodles, until just tender, in a large pan of rapidly boiling water, to which you have added 1 tsp salt and 1 tbsp olive oil. The time taken will depend on whether you use dried or fresh noodles, which are now readily available from most large supermarkets.

2. Meanwhile, make the sauce. Heat the remaining olive oil in a pan. Add the white parts from the chopped spring onions, reserving the green parts as a garnish, the strips of bacon, the garlic, if using, and salt and pepper to taste. Fry briefly for 3-4 minutes.

STEP 2

3. Stir in the baked beans and heat through.

4. Drain the cooked noodles and pile into a warmed serving dish. Top with the hot bean and bacon sauce and sprinkle with the reserved spring onion. Serve immediately, accompanied by the grated Parmesan cheese.

STEP 1

STEP 4

Cook's Notes

TIME: Preparation takes about 15 minutes and cooking takes 15-17 minutes.

? **VARIATION:** You could use different shaped pastas instead of the noodles.

SERVING IDEAS: For a more substantial meal, serve the dish with a mixed side salad.

BUYING GUIDE: If green noodles are not available, use ordinary noodles.

SPICY PASTA WITH PRAWNS

SERVES 4

A pasta dish with a difference – a delicious and spicy combination of mushrooms, prawns and Heinz Curried Beans with Sultanas served with pasta shells.

225g/8oz pasta shells
Salt
1 tbsp olive oil
2 x 225g/7.94oz cans Heinz Curried Beans with
    Sultanas
150ml/¼ pint single cream
100g/4oz peeled prawns
75g/3oz button mushrooms, thinly sliced
2 tbsps chopped parsley

1. Cook the pasta shells in a large pan of rapidly boiling water, to which you have added 1 tsp salt and the olive oil. Cook, until the pasta shells are just tender. The length of cooking time will depend on the size of shells chosen.

STEP 1

2. Meanwhile, make the sauce. Put the curried beans into a pan with the cream, prawns, button mushrooms, parsley and salt, to taste. It should not be necessary to add pepper, because of the curry sauce with the beans. Heat through gently.

STEP 2

3. Drain the cooked pasta shells thoroughly and pile into a warmed serving dish. Top with the hot sauce and serve immediately.

Cook's Notes

⌐ TIME: Preparation takes about 10 minutes and cooking takes about 15 minutes.

❗ WATCHPOINT: Do not heat the sauce for too long or at too high a temperature or the prawns will become tough.

◯ SERVING IDEAS: Serve this dish with a crisp green salad.

TURKEY BEAN BAKE

SERVES 3-4

There's no need to waste leftover turkey, when you can make this nourishing recipe from Heinz.

50g/2oz margarine
50g/2oz plain flour
575ml/1 pint milk
225g/8oz cooked turkey meat, chopped
1 x 450g/15.9oz can Heinz Baked Beans
100g/4oz pasta twists, cooked
100g/4oz Cheddar cheese, grated
2 large tomatoes, sliced
25g/1oz flaked almonds

1. Melt the margarine in a large pan. Remove the pan from the heat and stir in the flour, then blend in the milk gradually, to make a smooth sauce. Return the pan to the heat and, stirring continuously, bring the sauce to the boil.

STEP 1

2. Add the turkey meat and cook the mixture for 3 minutes. Stir in the beans and the cooked pasta, together with three quarters of the cheese. Season well.

STEP 2

STEP 2

3. Turn the mixture into a 1 litre/³/₄ pint, shallow ovenproof dish. Arrange the tomato slices on top and scatter over the almonds and the remaining cheese.

4. If the dish is to be served immediately, place it under the grill to brown. Alternatively, the dish may be left in a cool place, until required, when it should be put in a preheated oven, 180°C/350°F/Gas Mark 4, for 45 minutes.

Cook's Notes

↳ TIME: Preparation takes about 15 minutes and cooking also takes about 15 minutes.

! WATCHPOINT: Blend the milk into the sauce very gradually or the sauce will become lumpy.

? VARIATION: You could try various types of cheese for different flavour combinations.

BEANZ LASAGNE

SERVES 4

Heinz offers you a tasty, nourishing variation on this traditional Italian recipe – ideal for children's meals.

50g/2oz butter, or margarine
1 large onion, chopped
225g/8oz minced beef
1 x 450g/15.9oz can Heinz Baked Beans
2 tbsps tomato purée
Salt and pepper
8 sheets lasagne
25g/1oz plain flour
275ml/½ pint milk
Ground nutmeg
50g/2oz Cheddar cheese, grated

---

1. Melt half the butter and fry the onion in it, until soft. Add the minced beef and brown it well. Stir in the beans and the tomato purée and season well. Simmer for 5 minutes.

STEP 1

2. Cook the lasagne in boiling water, as directed on the packet.

3. Melt the remaining butter, add the flour and cook for 2 minutes, stirring. Add the milk gradually and bring to the boil, stirring continuously. Simmer for 2 minutes, then season the sauce well with a pinch of nutmeg and salt and pepper.

4. Grease an ovenproof dish and arrange two sheets of lasagne on the base. Spoon over a quarter of the bean and beef mixture and a quarter of the sauce. Repeat 3 more times, until all the ingredients have been used up.

STEP 4

STEP 4

5. Sprinkle the lasagne with the grated cheese and bake in a preheated oven, 180°C/350°F/ Gas Mark 4, for 30 minutes, until golden and bubbling.

Cook's Notes

TIME: Preparation takes about 30 minutes and cooking takes about 1½ hours.

VARIATION: You could use the green, spinach-flavoured lasagne sheets to ring the changes.

SERVING IDEAS: To make a more substantial meal, serve the lasagne dish with a green salad or a vegetable.

BEAN AND MEAT LOAF

SERVES 4

Baked beans team up well with minced meat, adding flavour and succulence and helping to make a little meat go a long way. This recipe makes the most of both in a hearty dish that's perfect for cold nights.

1 small onion, finely chopped
1 clove garlic, crushed
1 red pepper, seeded and finely chopped
350g/12oz minced beef
75g/3oz fresh breadcrumbs
Salt and freshly ground black pepper
1 x 450g/15.9oz can Heinz Baked Beans
2 tbsps chopped parsley
1 egg, beaten
3 rashers lean bacon

1. Combine the onion, garlic, red pepper, minced beef, breadcrumbs and seasoning in a large bowl and mix well.

STEP 1

2. Drain the baked beans and add to the meat mixture. Mix in the parsley and beaten egg and set to one side.

3. Line the base and sides of a lightly greased loaf tin with the bacon rashers. Spoon the prepared mixture into the tin and smooth the top level.

STEP 3

STEP 3

4. Cover with a piece of greased foil. Bake at 180°C/350°F/Gas Mark 4 for 45-50 minutes. Leave in the tin for a few minutes, before turning out. Serve with fresh tomato sauce, if liked.

Cook's Notes

⌚ TIME: Preparation takes about 15 minutes and cooking takes about 45-50 minutes.

◆ PREPARATION: If red pepper is unavailable, use a tin of pimentos.

✳ FREEZING: Prepare the meat loaf in advance and freeze, before cooking. Freeze in the tin, label and store for up to one month. Allow to defrost completely, before cooking as above.

CHINESE-STYLE BEANS AND SAUSAGES

SERVES 4

This exciting mixture of oriental ingredients, such as bean sprouts, soy sauce and ginger, and Heinz Baked Beans with Pork Sausages creates an unusual and tasty dish.

1 medium onion, chopped
2 tbsps oil
1 clove garlic, chopped
1 red pepper, seeded and cut into thin strips
2 x 450g/15.9oz cans Heinz Baked Beans with
    Pork Sausages
¼ tsp ground ginger
100g/4oz button mushrooms, thinly sliced
4 tbsps fresh bean sprouts, lightly cooked, or
    drained, canned bean sprouts
1 tbsp soy sauce
2 tbsps roasted cashew nuts
Salt and freshly ground black pepper
1 tbsp chopped fresh coriander or parsley

1. Fry the onion gently in the oil for 3 minutes. Add the garlic and red pepper and fry gently for a further 3 minutes.

STEP 1

2. Add the baked beans with pork sausages, ginger, mushrooms, bean sprouts, soy sauce, cashew nuts and salt and pepper to taste. Heat through.

STEP 2

3. Spoon into a warmed serving dish and sprinkle with the coriander, or parsley. Serve as an accompaniment to cooked rice, pasta and vegetable dishes.

Cook's Notes

TIME: Preparation takes about 15 minutes and cooking takes a further 10 minutes.

VARIATION: You could substitute chestnuts for the cashew nuts.

COOK'S TIP: If the mushrooms are clean, do not wash them. If they do require washing, rinse them quickly and pat dry, to prevent the mushrooms becoming soggy.

BEAN, KIDNEY AND PEPPER BAKE

SERVES 4

There's no need to eat only bland dishes, when you're on a diet. This Bean, Kidney and Pepper Bake from Heinz is full of flavour, but contains only 290 calories per portion. Serve with a crunchy salad, to complete the meal.

8 lambs' kidneys, skinned, cored and sliced
150ml/¼ pint chicken stock
Salt and freshly ground black pepper
1 medium onion, thinly sliced
1 tbsp oil
1 large red pepper, seeded and sliced
1 large green pepper, seeded and sliced
1 clove garlic, crushed
1 x 450g/15.9oz can Heinz Baked Beans
2 tomatoes, sliced
200ml/⅓ pint natural yogurt
2 eggs
50g/2oz cheese, grated

1. Put the sliced kidneys into a shallow pan with the chicken stock and salt and pepper to taste. Simmer gently, until the kidneys are just tender. Do not overcook them, as kidneys toughen easily.

2. Fry the onion gently in the oil for 3-4 minutes, preferably in a non-stick pan. Add the sliced red and green peppers and the garlic. Cover the pan and cook gently for 5 minutes.

3. Drain the kidneys and mix with the peppers and onion. Stir in the baked beans. Spoon into a shallow, greased gratin dish. Arrange the sliced tomatoes on top.

4. Beat the yogurt with the eggs, season to taste and spoon evenly over the vegetables, beans and kidneys. Sprinkle with the grated cheese

5. Bake at 190°/375°F/Gas Mark 5 for about 30 minutes, until the yogurt topping is golden and set. Serve piping hot.

Cook's Notes

TIME: Preparation takes about 25 minutes and cooking takes 45 minutes.

BUYING GUIDE: Kidneys quickly lose both their flavour and goodness and should be bought as fresh as possible. Their freshness is easier to judge if the kidneys are bought still encased in their fat.

HOME-STYLE BEANS WITH EGGS

SERVES 4

A protein-filled recipe from Heinz that makes an ideal vegetarian lunch or supper dish.

2 tbsps oil
100g/4oz onion, sliced
450g/1lb potatoes, cooked and diced
2 x 225g/7.94oz cans Heinz Curried Beans with
    Sultanas
Salt
4 eggs
50g/2oz Cheddar cheese, grated

1. Heat the oil in a flameproof casserole and fry the onion until transparent. Stir in the potatoes and curried beans and add salt to taste.

2. Make four 'nests' in the bean mixture and break an egg into each one.

3. Sprinkle with the grated cheese and bake in a preheated oven, 200°C/400°F/Gas Mark 6, for 15–20 minutes, until bubbling.

Cook's Notes

TIME: Preparation takes about 15 minutes and cooking takes 25 minutes.

SERVING IDEAS: Serve this dish with some crusty French bread for a satisfying meal.

VARIATION: Many different types of cheese could be used for this recipe; try a blue cheese for a stronger flavour.

BAKED MARROW SURPRISE

SERVES 4

Make the most of marrow with this delicious recipe from Heinz. It's a quick and easy idea for an informal supper party, or family lunch.

---

1 marrow, about 1kg/2¼lbs
350g/12oz minced beef
1 medium onion, finely chopped
1 tbsp tomato purée
1 x 450g/15.9oz can Heinz Baked Beans
2 tsps mixed herbs
4 tbsps porridge oats
Salt and pepper
1 orange, sliced

---

1. Cut a lid from one side of the marrow and scoop out all the seeds. Put the marrow shell onto a large piece of greased foil and leave it to one side.

STEP 1

2. Mix the minced beef with the onion, tomato purée, baked beans, herbs and porridge oats. Season the filling well, then pack it into the marrow shell.

STEP 2

3. Cut the lid into four pieces and replace it on the marrow, with the orange slices arranged in between.

STEP 3

4. Wrap the foil around the marrow completely, place the parcel in a roasting tin and bake at 200°C/400°F/Gas Mark 6 for about 1¼ hours, or until cooked. Serve with creamed potatoes.

Cook's Notes

⏱ TIME: Preparation takes about 15 minutes and cooking takes about 1¼ hours.

❓ VARIATION: If marrow is out of season, green peppers make a tasty alternative.

BEAN MOUSSAKA

SERVES 4-6

*Who put the baked beans in moussaka?
Certainly not the Greeks. Nevertheless, many
classic European dishes actually lend themselves
to the inclusion of baked beans which also
makes them more economical to prepare.*

1 large onion, chopped
3 tbsps olive oil, or other cooking oil
1 large clove garlic, crushed
350g/12oz lean, minced lamb
2 tbsps tomato purée
1 tsp dried oregano
2 x 450g/15.9oz cans Heinz Baked Beans
Salt and freshly ground black pepper
3 large potatoes, peeled and thinly sliced
100g/4oz Feta cheese, crumbled, or Cheddar
    cheese, grated (see note below)
150ml/¼ pint soured cream
150ml/¼ pint natural yogurt
2 eggs

NB: Feta is the Greek cheese usually used in
    moussaka. It can now be bought from most
    large supermarkets, but Cheddar can be
    used as a substitute.

1. Fry the chopped onion gently in the oil for
3-4 minutes. Add the garlic and minced lamb
and fry, until the meat is evenly browned.

2. Stir in the tomato purée, oregano, baked
beans and salt and pepper to taste. Simmer for 5
minutes.

3. Arrange one half of the meat and bean
mixture in a deep, greased ovenproof dish and
layer with a little of the cheese and half the
sliced potato.

4. Repeat with the remaining meat mixture, a
little more of the cheese and the remaining sliced
potato.

5. Beat the soured cream and yogurt with the
eggs and spoon evenly over the top layer of
potatoes. Sprinkle with the remaining cheese.
Bake at 190°C/375°F/Gas Mark 5 for 45-50
minutes, testing with a skewer, to ensure the
potatoes are cooked.

Cook's Notes

TIME: Preparation takes about 20
minutes and cooking takes about 1¼ hours.

VARIATION: For a stronger flavour, use
a red onion.

ECONOMY: This is a good dish for
using up leftover roast lamb, which should
be minced, before proceeding with the
recipe as above.

WINTER WARMING BEAN CASSEROLE

SERVES 4

For a warming change in winter, try this tasty pork and baked bean casserole from Heinz. The cider not only makes it deliciously moist, but adds a slightly unusual flavour.

775g/1lb 12oz pork spare ribs
450g/1lb swede
450g/1lb leeks
25g/1oz lard
225g/8oz cooking apples
275ml/½ pint dry cider
1 x 450g/15.9oz can Heinz Baked Beans

---

1. Trim the pork, removing any bones and excess fat, then cut the meat into 2.5cm/1 inch pieces. Peel and cube the swede. Remove any damaged leaves from the leeks, then trim the ends and wash them. Cut each leek into 2.5cm/1 inch pieces.

STEP 1

2. Melt the fat in a frying pan, add the meat and cook it until lightly browned, then transfer to a 2.5 litre/5 pint casserole dish.

3. Fry the swede and leeks gently for about 5 minutes, then add them to the meat.

4. Peel, core and slice the apples thickly. Add them to the casserole dish.

STEP 4

5. Pour over the cider, stir in the baked beans and season the casserole well.

STEP 5

6. Cook in a preheated oven, 180°C/350°F/Gas Mark 4, for 1½ hours, or until the meat is tender. Serve with jacket potatoes, baked in the oven along with the casserole.

Cook's Notes

⏱ TIME: Preparation takes about 30 minutes and cooking takes about 2 hours.

◣ PREPARATION: Use some of the excess fat trimmed from the spare ribs to fry the meat. This enhances the flavour of the casserole.

❗ WATCHPOINT: Add the cider to the casserole gradually, or it may foam up and boil over.

❓ VARIATION: Any winter vegetables may be used in the casserole, as preferred.

QUICK BEAN CASSOULET

SERVES 6

Cassoulet is a haricot bean stew, which comes from the Languedoc region of France. This classic dish takes a long time to prepare and cook, but a quick and easy variation can be made using Heinz Baked Beans.

1 thick slice smoked bacon, about 175g/6oz in weight, cubed
350g/12oz pork fillet, cubed
1 leek, sliced
1 large carrot, thickly sliced
1 small onion, sliced
1 tbsp chopped fresh thyme
Freshly ground black pepper
2 cloves garlic, finely chopped
425ml/³/₄ pint chicken stock
12 rashers streaky bacon
2 x 450g/15.9oz cans Heinz Baked Beans
175g/6oz garlic sausage, cut into small cubes
2 tbsps chopped parsley
4 tomatoes, skinned, seeded and chopped
4 tbsps dried breadcrumbs

1. Put the cubed bacon, pork fillet, leek, carrot, onion and thyme into a pan. Add pepper to taste, half the garlic and the stock. Cover the pan, bring to the boil and simmer, until the meats are almost tender. Drain the meats and vegetables, reserving the stock.

STEP 1

2. Line the base and sides of an earthenware casserole with eight of the bacon rashers.

STEP 2

3. Mix the baked beans with the remaining garlic, pepper to taste, garlic sausage and parsley.

STEP 3

4. Spoon half the bean mixture into the casserole. Top with the meat and vegetable mixture and the chopped tomatoes. Add the remaining bean mixture. Spoon over about 4 tbsps of the meat cooking stock and lay the remaining four bacon rashers over the top.

5. Cover the casserole and cook in a preheated oven, 180°C/350°F/Gas Mark 4, for 45 minutes. Remove the lid, sprinkle the top of the cassoulet with breadcrumbs and return to the oven for a further 15 minutes, uncovered.

Cook's Notes

TIME: Preparation takes about 40 minutes and cooking takes about 2½ hours.

PREPARATION: The casserole may be prepared in advance and reheated prior to serving.

VARIATION: Other seasonal vegetables may used, as desired, but root vegetables should always be cooked first.

SPICED LAMB AND BEAN RISOTTO

SERVES 4

A spicy risotto from Heinz, which is quick to prepare and ideal for an informal supper party.

450g/1lb shoulder of lamb, excess fat removed
1 medium onion, chopped
275ml/¹/₂ pint water
1 chicken stock cube
2 medium carrots, peeled
100g/4oz long grain rice
2 x 225g/7.94oz cans Heinz Curried Beans with
    Sultanas
4 tbsps parsley, or mint, chopped
Salt

1. Cut the meat into very small pieces and place it in a saucepan with the onion. Cook over a medium heat, stirring continuously until the meat is coloured.

2. Add the water and the stock cube, cover and simmer for 20 minutes.

3. Dice the carrots roughly and add to the pan with the rice. Stir well, cover and simmer for 15 minutes. Stir frequently during cooking.

4. Add the beans and parsley and a little extra water, if necessary. Heat through for 5 more minutes. Check flavour and adjust the seasoning to taste.

Cook's Notes

TIME: Preparation takes about 30 minutes and cooking takes about 1 hour.

VARIATION: You could substitute dry white wine for half the chicken stock.

WATCHPOINT: The risotto should be stirred frequently and more liquid added, if it begins to dry out.

FREEZING: After cooking the risotto, cool it completely and transfer to an airtight container. Label and freeze for up to 3 months.

AUBERGINES PROVENÇALE

SERVES 4

Aubergines, minced meat and baked beans combine to create this delicious variation on a classic French dish.

---

2 large aubergines
Salt and freshly ground black pepper
1 medium onion, chopped
2 tbsps oil
350g/12oz minced beef
175g/6oz button mushrooms, chopped
1 clove garlic, chopped
275ml/½ pint red wine
2 tbsps tomato purée
1 x 450g/15.9oz can Heinz Baked Beans
1 x 425g/14oz can peeled tomatoes, drained and sieved
1 tbsp chopped parsley

---

1. Cut each aubergine in half lengthways. Score the cut surface of the flesh lightly at regular intervals and sprinkle generously with salt. Leave to drain upside down for 30 minutes.

STEP 1

2. Wipe the cut surface of each half aubergine. Carefully hollow out the centre flesh, leaving 4 aubergine shells, about 1cm/½ inch thick. Chop the centre flesh roughly.

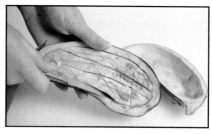

STEP 2

3. Fry the onion in the oil for 3-4 minutes. Add the minced beef and cook until evenly browned. Add the chopped aubergine flesh, mushrooms, garlic, salt and pepper to taste, and half the red wine. Simmer gently for 10-15 minutes.

4. Stir in the tomato purée. Drain the baked beans, reserving the sauce. Add the beans to the meat mixture. Spoon the meat and bean filling into each aubergine shell and stand them, upright, in a lightly greased, ovenproof dish. Cover with greased foil and bake at 190°C/375°F/Gas Mark 5 for 40 minutes. Remove the foil and return to the oven for a further 5-10 minutes.

5. Meanwhile, make the sauce. Put the remaining red wine into a pan with the reserved bean sauce, the sieved tomatoes, parsley and salt and pepper to taste. Put the cooked, stuffed aubergines into a serving dish and spoon the hot sauce over the top. Serve immediately.

Cook's Notes

TIME: Preparation takes about 30 minutes and cooking takes about 1 hour 10 minutes.

COOK'S TIP: It is advisable to salt and drain the aubergines as described, because this helps eliminate the bitter flavour normally associated with these vegetables.

TACOS WITH BEEF AND BEANS

SERVES 6

Mexican food is fun to prepare, colourful to look at and delicious to eat and one of the staple ingredients is beans The Mexicans use pinto beans, we use Heinz!

6 ready-made taco shells (see note below)
1 small onion, finely chopped
2 tbsps oil
350g/12oz minced beef
2 green peppers, seeded and finely chopped
2 tbsps taco sauce (see note below)
4 tbsps red wine
Salt and freshly ground black pepper
1 x 450g/15.9oz can Heinz Baked Beans

To Garnish
Extra taco sauce
Extra chopped green pepper
6 plump, black olives

NB: Taco shells and sauce, together with other Mexican foods, can now be purchased from most large supermarkets. Taco shells are cup-shaped, corn dough pancakes, which have been fried until crisp.

1. Put the taco shells onto a baking sheet.

STEP 1

2. Fry the chopped onion gently in the oil for 3-4 minutes. Add the minced beef and fry, until evenly browned. Add the chopped green peppers, taco sauce, red wine and salt and pepper, to taste. Simmer gently, until the beef is just tender. The mixture should be fairly 'dry'.

STEP 2

3. Add the baked beans and heat through.

4. Warm the taco shells in the oven, according to the instructions on the packet.

5. Fill each warmed taco shell with the hot bean and beef mixture. Garnish with the extra taco sauce, chopped green pepper and the olives and serve immediately.

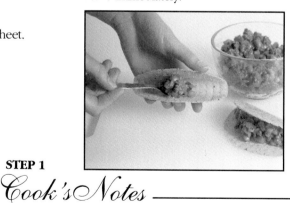

STEP 5

Cook's Notes

? VARIATION: Instead of using just green peppers, use red or yellow, either on their own or mixed.

↳ TIME: Preparation takes about 20 minutes and cooking takes about 30 minutes.

▣ COOK'S TIP: The filled taco shells are best served immediately, as they may become soggy otherwise.

PORK AND BEAN STROGANOFF

SERVES 4

Not only do beans help to make a meal, but they also help to make some of the more expensive ingredients go that little bit further. This Pork and Bean Stroganoff is equally suitable for family meals or for entertaining.

1 medium onion, finely chopped
25g/1oz butter
1 tbsp oil
450g/1lb pork fillet, cut into thin strips
Seasoned flour
200ml/⅓ pint chicken stock, or dry white wine
1 clove garlic, crushed
100g/4oz button mushrooms, left whole if small, or sliced
1 tbsp chopped chives
1 x 450/15.9oz can Heinz Baked Beans
Dry sherry and soured cream (optional)

1. Fry the onion gently in the butter and oil for 3 minutes. Dust the pork strips in the seasoned flour and add them to the hot fat. Fry, until sealed and lightly coloured on all sides.

2. Stir in the stock and the garlic and bring to the boil. Add the mushrooms and simmer gently for 12-15 minutes, until the pork is tender.

3. Stir in the chives and baked beans and heat through. Serve piping hot with cooked noodles or rice. If desired, a little dry sherry and some soured cream may be stirred into the dish immediately prior to serving.

STEP 3

STEP 1

Cook's Notes

TIME: Preparation takes about 15 minutes and cooking takes about 25-30 minutes.

VARIATION: Other lean cuts of meat, such as lamb or beef, can be used instead of the pork.

FREEZING: After cooking the stroganoff, allow to cool completely and transfer it to an airtight container. Label and freeze for up to 3 months.

PRAWN AND BEAN PILAFF

SERVES 4

When you want the spiciness of a curry, try this appetising bean and rice dish.

1 medium onion, finely chopped
3 tbsps olive oil, or cooking oil
175g/6oz long grain rice
275ml/½ pint dry white wine
425ml/¾ pint chicken stock
2 x 225g/7.94oz cans Heinz Curried Beans
175g/6oz peeled prawns
Salt and freshly ground black pepper

1. Fry the onion gently in the oil for 3-4 minutes. Add the rice and stir over a gentle heat, until the rice is evenly coated with oil.

2. Stir in the white wine gradually. Bring to the boil and simmer gently, until the wine has been absorbed.

3. Stir in 275ml/½ pint of the chicken stock gradually and simmer gently, until the stock has been absorbed. Add the remaining stock and continue cooking the rice, until it is tender and all the liquid has been absorbed.

4. Stir in the curried beans, the peeled prawns and salt and pepper to taste. Heat through. Serve with a simple cucumber and yogurt salad. If desired, a few cooked peas can be added to the pilaff at the same time as the curried beans and the prawns.

Cook's Notes

TIME: Preparation takes about 15 minutes and cooking takes about 25-30 minutes.

WATCHPOINT: Do not heat the prawns for too long or at too high a temperature, as they toughen easily.

VARIATION: A few diced, cooked vegetables may be added to the dish, if desired.

EXOTIC WINTER SALAD

SERVES 4

For a really tasty, main-meal salad with lots of visual appeal, try this Heinz recipe. At only 325 calories per portion, approximately, it's good news for slimmers, too.

1 x 450g/15.9oz can Heinz Baked Beans
Grated rind and juice of ½ a large orange
2 tbsps chopped parsley, or chives
1 clove garlic, crushed
3 spring onions, chopped
4 large tomatoes, seeded and chopped
3 sticks celery, chopped
1 ripe avocado pear, peeled, stoned and
    chopped
½ small head Chinese leaves, or ½ small white
    cabbage
175g/6oz curd cheese, or cottage cheese, sieved
Salt and freshly ground black pepper
Paprika, or finely chopped parsley
Peeled segments from 1 large orange

1. Mix the beans with the orange rind and juice.

2. Stir in the parsley, garlic, spring onions, chopped tomatoes, celery and avocado pear.

3. Shred the Chinese leaves, or cabbage, quite finely and arrange on a flat serving dish.

4. Mix the curd cheese, or sieved cottage cheese, with salt and pepper to taste, and form into small balls, about the size of a grape. Roll these in paprika, or chopped parsley, to coat evenly.

5. Spoon the bean and vegetable mixture on top of the Chinese leaves, or cabbage. Garnish with the cheese balls and the orange segments.

Cook's Notes

TIME: Preparation takes about 30 minutes.

COOK'S TIP: After peeling and chopping the avocado, coat it with lemon juice to prevent discolouration.

VARIATION: A variety of fresh herbs may be used instead of those suggested, as preferred. Any other citrus fruit may be substituted for the orange.

BEAN CHEESECAKE

SERVES 6-8

When it comes to packing a picnic basket, most people are stuck for original ideas. A Bean Cheesecake may sound unusual, but it tastes delicious and makes a pleasant alternative to the more standard quiche, sandwiches or sausage rolls. If the cheesecake is made in a loose-bottomed cake tin, as suggested, it can be transported very easily.

STEP 2

Base
100g/4oz water biscuits, finely crushed
1 tbsp poppy seeds
50g/2oz melted butter

Filling
225g/8oz cream cheese
275ml/¹/₂ pint soured cream
2 eggs
1 x 450g/15.9oz can Heinz Baked Beans
Salt and freshly ground black pepper
1 clove garlic, crushed
25g/1oz powdered gelatine
5 tbsps water

Garnish
Sliced cucumber
Sliced, or whole olives, either pitted black ones
    or stuffed green ones
Paprika

1. Lightly grease or oil a 20cm/8 inch, loose-bottomed cake tin.

2. To make the base, mix the crushed water biscuits with the poppy seeds and the melted butter. Press the biscuit mixture evenly over the base of the tin. Chill for 30 minutes.

3. To make the filling, put the cream cheese into the liquidiser, together with the soured cream, eggs, baked beans, salt and pepper to taste and the garlic. Blend until smooth.

4. Dissolve the powdered gelatine in the water and stir evenly into the cheese and bean mixture. Pour this into the prepared tin.

STEP 4

5. Chill the savoury cheesecake, until the filling has set. Decorate the top with the sliced cucumber and olives and sprinkle with paprika.

6. To serve, lift the set cheesecake out, on its base, and serve cut into wedges with a salad.

Cook's Notes

TIME: Preparation takes about 40 minutes plus a minimum of 4 hours chilling time.

PREPARATION: If the base mixture is too dry, add more melted butter.

COOK'S TIP: Before lifting out the cheesecake, loosen its edges from the tin using a spatula.

VARIATION: If you use digestive biscuits, instead of water biscuits, the cheesecake will have a sweeter taste.

CAESAR BEAN SALAD

SERVES 4

Baked beans make a tasty change from the more usual salad vegetables, which can become very monotonous. Here they are used to provide a variation on a traditional salad dish.

1 x 450g/15.9oz can Heinz Baked Beans
Juice of ½ a lemon
Salt and freshly ground black pepper
2 tsps Worcestershire sauce
2 cloves garlic, crushed
1 egg
5 tbsps olive oil
2 crustless slices of bread, cut into small cubes
1 small iceberg lettuce, shredded
1 head chicory, shredded
75g/3oz French beans, lightly cooked
12 black olives
Parsley, or chives, chopped

1. Drain the baked beans thoroughly in a sieve. Keep the beans to one side.

STEP 1

2. Mix the bean juice with the lemon juice, salt and pepper to taste, Worcestershire sauce and 1 of the crushed garlic cloves. Soft-boil the egg in boiling water for 45 seconds. Crack the shell carefully and scoop the liquid egg into the dressing. Beat these ingredients together well with a fork, adding 2 tbsps of the olive oil.

STEP 2

3. Heat the remaining oil in a shallow pan with the other clove of crushed garlic. Add the bread cubes and fry, until lightly golden.

STEP 3

4. Put the shredded lettuce, chicory, French beans and black olives into a bowl. Add the drained baked beans and the fried bread cubes and toss lightly together, taking care not to break up the beans.

5. Add the prepared dressing to the salad and toss lightly. Divide the salad between individual serving dishes, garnish with chopped parsley, or chives, and serve.

Cook's Notes

TIME: Preparation takes about 20-25 minutes. Cooking the croutons takes about 5 minutes.

PREPARATION: Wash the chicory quickly, as soaking intensifies its bitter taste, and then brush the leaves with lemon juice, to prevent discolouration.

VARIATION: For a more colourful salad, use red chicory. There is no difference in taste between this and the white chicory.

INDEX